Shakti Girls

Poems of Inspiring Indian Women

Written by Shetal Shah

Illustrated by Kavita Rajput

To all the girls I have taught,
you continue to inspire me.
And to my parents:
without your sacrifice, my dream to write this book would not exist.
- S.S.

For my mother, Manisha Aras, the first Shakti Girl I knew.
- K.R.

SHAKTI GIRLS, LLC
Atlanta, USA

Title Art copyright © 2022 Shakti Girls LLC
Text copyright © 2022 Shetal Shah
Illustrations copyright © 2022 Kavita Rajput
All rights reserved, including the right of reproduction in whole or in part in any form.
For more information and bulk orders, please contact Shetal Shah at shetalshahauthor@gmail.com.
Book design by Kavita Rajput
The text for this book is set in Quicksand.
The illustrations for this book are rendered using pencil, watercolors and Procreate.
ISBN: 979-8-9869545-1-6

Thank you, Abi, for your prowess in editing and supporting this book. Thanks to all my family, and friends, including Aishani, Armaan, Asha, Avi, Jayen, Maggie, and Shalini for your feedback and enthusiasm. - S.S.

Shakti: The power and energy within you

In traditional Hinduism, the word "shakti" refers to the power and energy that creates and maintains the universe. This energy is female, as it is mothers who have the power to give birth to new life.

Your shakti can appear in many different ways. It can appear as music, art, dance, athletics, or intelligence.

There is shakti in all of us.
What is your shakti?

ASHA BHOSLE
Singing Queen
Born September 8, 1933
Maharashtra, India

Her voice adds life to any Hindi song—
tap to the beat, and you can sing along!

Trained by her father with music in his heart,
she and her *behen* showed promise in this art.

When tragedy struck, her family took flight.
To help them all out, she found the spotlight.

For years, she lived in her sister's shadow,
working hard to find her hit solo.

And when she did, no one was surprised—
her talent to sing was no compromise!

Her harmony lifts listeners to the clouds,
filling their ears with light and no doubt:

the first Indian Grammy nominee
means clearly Asha's talent is uncanny!

A Guinness Book of World Records holder,
for the most recordings, there's no one bolder.

A business owner, chef, and music queen,
Asha's breadth of pursuits are unforeseen.

An example of strength, hard work, and fruition,
she shows your *sapane* can come true with ambition.

DO YOU KNOW THESE WORDS?
Behen: Sister in Hindi
Fruition: Accomplishment; when a plan happens
Pursuits: Activities
Sapane: Dreams in Hindi
Uncanny: Superhuman

CAN YOU FIND THESE OBJECTS?
Music notes - 3
Grammy Trophy
Headphones

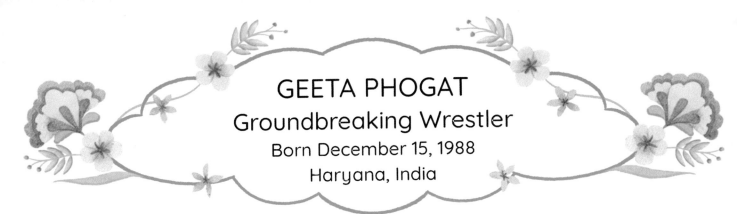

GEETA PHOGAT
Groundbreaking Wrestler
Born December 15, 1988
Haryana, India

In a country where wrestling was only for men,
Geeta defied all odds as a top ten.

From a village in Haryana, her hometown,
she studied and practiced till sundown.

Her father, former wrestler—and coach too!—
was thrilled to train Geeta, although taboo.

A strict practice schedule, it's hard to believe:
every day, including Sunday, you see . . .

When it's frigid! Blazing! In all kinds of air!
In mud pits! With bricks as weights to prepare!

Ignoring taunts and teasing by neighbors,
she stayed *hathee* when they didn't see her.

Years of hard work finally turned into gold
at the Commonwealth Games—Geeta was bold!

India's first female wrestler at the Summer Olympics,
she continued with Worlds and put bronze in the mix.

The hit film *Dangal* spread Geeta's story:
that girls can rise to all kinds of glory,

changing the view towards women and sports
from the wrestling ring to the basketball court.

Don't be afraid to wrestle with something new—
go master a skill that makes your heart true!

DO YOU KNOW THESE WORDS?
Defied: Refused to obey
Taboo: Behavior that is considered unacceptable
Hathee: Headstrong in Hindi

CAN YOU FIND THESE OBJECTS?
Bricks
Indian flag
Wrestling clubbell

INDIRA GANDHI
India's Iron Lady
Born November 19, 1917 | Died October 31, 1984
Uttar Pradesh, India

A powerful prime minister and pioneer,
Indira's bold *avaaz* the world would hear.

Born in India under British rule—
her father, Nehru, sparked political fuel.

From the start, she immersed in all politics,
Acting for change and a country-wide fix.

She played the same games as her cousin-brothers
and ignored gender norms, one after the other.

Fighting for India's freedom early on,
she showed her dissent that she acted upon:

rejecting British goods, a protesting act—
she burned her English doll to make an impact.

Prime minister: her goal (and a sight to see)
in '66 became her reality!

Some asked, "A puppet for those underneath?"
Turns out, her leadership had grit and teeth.

While much of her work is argued today,
helping the poor was a key point conveyed.

Ensuring food for the poor and the hungry,
she improved farming tools in her country.

"Iron Lady of India" was her nickname.
She made a global power—no small claim to fame!

A path into politics she blazed ahead.
What path will you take so your ideas spread?

DO YOU KNOW THESE WORDS?
Avaaz: Voice in Hindi
Immersed: Deeply involved
Dissent: Having a different opinion
Grit: Courage

CAN YOU FIND THESE OBJECTS?
Outline of India
Tractor
Ashoka Chakra (India's Flag Wheel) - 4

INDRA NOOYI
Corporate Trailblazer
Born October 28, 1955
Tamil Nadu, India

A chairwoman and a corporate star,
Indra lit paths that take others far.

Raised in Chennai, her beloved hometown,
she became a rebel who learned to never look down.

Her parents believed that all girls can soar,
to pursue what they want and let their voice roar.

"Pretend you are president!" Ma would say.
"Follow your *vishvaas* in every way!"

Yale business school drew her to the US,
where she climbed executive ranks with success.

She became the first woman to lead PepsiCo—
the first immigrant to lead a Fortune 500, you know!

Indra was anxious at first as a new CEO
but took confidence in her research for growth.

Performance with Purpose, a plan she designed,
promoted good health. Care for Earth she outlined.

By taking a stand with Pepsi this way,
she doubled sales and made global cachet.

An inductee of the Women's Hall of Fame,
the one and only Indra is there—her name

reminds us all to love in who we are.
With faith and will, you can raise the bar.

DO YOU KNOW THESE WORDS?
Vishvaas: Confidence, faith in Hindi
Cachet: Prestige, recognition
Inductee: A person officially accepted into a group

CAN YOU FIND THESE OBJECTS?
Dollar Sign - 3
Pepsico Logo
Stars - 2

JHUMPA LAHIRI
Award-Winning Writer
Born July 11, 1967
London, England

One of the world's most respected authors,
Jhumpa writes stories of many like her:

tales of American-*desi* identity,
challenges of both tugging at reality.

Unable to pronounce her proper name,
teachers called her by the family nickname.

Nilanjana, meaning "one with blue eyes,"
merges two worlds on the page (though it's hard in real life).

Her novel, *Namesake*, describes this life of two:
pressure to be fluent in both old and new.

Writing stories that reflect lives of immigrants,
she gives voice to those faced with such predicaments.

She won a Pulitzer Prize for her fiction—
for storytelling and her poetic diction.

Her passion for languages grew over time;
Italian offered other lingual design.

Jhumpa's stories have helped so many be seen
through the *satya* of life in two worlds and between.

Her voice inspires writers South Asian
to rouse and spark their diverse imaginations.

So share your story; it deserves to be told.
Grab a pencil and let your ideas unfold!

DO YOU KNOW THESE WORDS?
Desi: People of India in Hindi
Fluent: To speak and write easily and accurately
Predicament: A difficult situation
Satya: Truth in Hindi
Rouse: Awaken

CAN YOU FIND THESE OBJECTS?
Pulitzer Prize
Pen
Medal

KALPANA CHAWLA
Legendary Astronaut
Born March 17, 1962 | Died February 1, 2003
Haryana, India

With airplanes and rockets among the bright moon and stars,
Kalpana went to space and journeyed so far!

Born in Haryana, nicknamed "Montu,"
"Kalpana" she picked—"creative," it's true!

Delighted by planes as a young child,
she and her father watched them fly in style.

She loved aeronautics—her major in college—
despite hearing "for girls, it's useless knowledge."

She stayed strong in her goals and moved to the US
to earn a PhD (wondrous, no less!).

Now Dr. Chawla, astronaut for NASA,
had her first mission, left the whole world in awe.

With hundreds of orbits and hours in space,
she's the first Indian woman in a cosmic place!

Her impact on Earth was felt far and wide:
girls' summers at NASA, a gift she'd provide.

Her second trip on the Shuttle ended tragically—
she is now remembered heroically:

A Congressional Space Medal of Honor,
schools in her name, her impact made longer.

She taught all girls, Be *nidar* of trying,
stretch to new heights, and dream of flying.

DO YOU KNOW THESE WORDS?
Aeronautics: The science of traveling through air
Nidar: Fearless in Hindi

CAN YOU FIND THESE OBJECTS?
Rocket
NASA Badge
Astronaut

KAMALA HARRIS
Madam Vice President
Born October 20, 1964
California, USA

Making history with a shattered glass ceiling,
Kamala's civic success is quite appealing!

Born in California to immigrant parents—
Jamaican and Indian—their values inherent,

passionate on issues of civil rights.
(They'd protest with her in a stroller till night!)

Raised to value her dual identity,
She embraced temple and church equally.

Kamala's grandparents she'd see in Chennai;
they shaped her on issues, on being an ally.

At thirteen, her passions fought injustice.
"Let the kids play!" she argued and accomplished!

She majored in law in college and beyond,
then became a lawyer, an advocate, and so on.

Described as *kathor*, wanting to do more,
she ran and won the race for senator.

She became the forty-ninth vice president!
The first Asian and Black woman, she represents

an author and voice for many inflamed,
one of the most powerful women she's named.

A true symbol of the American Dream,
Kamala's *achieved*—no matter how hard it seemed.

A true story of not letting limits get in one's way...
Your intellect, your drive is what truly gets a say.

DO YOU KNOW THESE WORDS?
Civic: Duties, activities of a town or city
Inherent: Belongs in one's nature; habit
Kathor: Tough in Hindi
Inflamed: Having strong feelings

CAN YOU FIND THESE OBJECTS?
Bald Eagle seal
US Flag - 3
Lotus flowers (Meaning of Kamala)

KASTURBA GANDHI
Freedom Fighter
Born April 11, 1869 | Died February 22, 1944
Gujarat, India

Inspiring freedom and a world more just,
Kasturba's an activist who promoted trust.

Born in 1869 in Gujarat
(when the British ruled—the unjust autocrats!),

she then married the "Mahatma," the "great soul."
Overshadowed, *her* story makes India whole!

She had no schooling, could not read or write,
but her *chaturai* proved that she was bright!

All through her life, she used her loud voice,
teaching that women can make their own choice.

When in South Africa, Kasturba found unfairness,
so she spoke up for change and social progress.

She was arrested for protesting bad laws—
laws treating Hindus unfairly, she saw!

Inspired *satyagraha* (fair advocacy),
she resisted with peace and equality.

She went back to India—now time to do more,
to fight for freedom and open a new door.

She never saw the fruits of her labor,
but her lessons on truth today are still favored.

India won! Became a free nation!
Proving satyagraha leads to salvation.

Her story inspires to get involved,
How will you take a stand, seek justice, and problem-solve?

DO YOU KNOW THESE WORDS?
Autocrat: A ruler who has absolute power
Chaturai: Cleverness in Hindi
Satyagraha: Peaceful resistance by holding onto truth
Salvation: Being saved

CAN YOU FIND THESE OBJECTS?
Peace symbol - 2
Equal Sign - 2
Charkha (Spinning Wheel)

MINDY KALING
Star Producer and Creator
Born June 24, 1979
Massachusetts, USA

Creative, witty, artistic, and bright,
Mindy fills rooms with laughter and delight!

A child of immigrants—Tamil and Bengali—
She's a voice for those who celebrate Diwali.

Raised near Boston, with a love for the arts
and a real *josh* for writing right from the start,

she learned to navigate two worlds split
Indian and American—but for her, close-knit.

At times unsure where her background fit in,
for being different, Hindu-American.

She majored in playwriting at Dartmouth College,
fed her passion with experience and knowledge.

A stand-up comic, she was one of few!
A strong woman of color, she pushed through.

Her break in acting was her main cue,
and she joined *The Office* as a writer, too!

Now a writer, producer, and actor,
she graces the screen in so many factors.

A pioneer and star in Hollywood,
creating her own show (no one else could),

breaking stereotypes, proving no one's the same—
she's lifted South Asians with talent to claim.

With resolve and grit, can't you see it?
Follow *your* passion and you can be it!

DO YOU KNOW THESE WORDS?
Diwali: Hindu festival of lights
Josh: Passion in Hindi
Stereotype: An often unfair and untrue belief about many people

CAN YOU FIND THESE OBJECTS?
Drama Masks - 2
Pen - 2
Diya (Indian Earthen lamp) - 2

MOHINI BHARDWAJ
World-Class Gymnast
Born September 29, 1978
Pennsylvania, USA

From balance on beams to spins on the floor,
watch how Mohini makes gymnastics soar!

The first Indian-American Olympic gymnast,
Mohini shows with *dhairya*, there is no limit.

With her backwards roll and effortless headstand,
natural talent was in clear command.

Born in Philly, then raised in Cincinnati,
at thirteen she trained in Houston and Miami.

Unafraid to blaze her own gymnast trail,
she stayed Hindu vegetarian *sans* fail.

Her passion for the sport never wavered
despite some setbacks that life ill-favored . . .

Truly resilient, with vision and dreams,
Mo worked jobs and trained—as hard as *that* seems!

Many days and nights of tears and sweat,
She became Team USA captain—no regrets.

While others trained with repetition and precision,
yoga and weight work were Mohini's decisions.

A solid performance on vault and floor . . .
Then a last-minute show on beam with high scores!

A silver medal! Now the world knew her name.
Next? USA Gymnastics Hall of Fame!

A true athlete can look different ways.
With work and will, you too can seize the day.

DO YOU KNOW THESE WORDS?
Dhairya: Strength, endurance in Hindi
Resilient: Ability to recover quickly

CAN YOU FIND THESE OBJECTS?
Balance Beam
Olympic rings
Silver Medal

MOTHER TERESA
Altruistic Caregiver
Born August 26, 1910 | Died September 5, 1997
Skopje, Macedonia

A great humanitarian of our time,
She helped the poor and sick—a true divine.

Born in Macedonia (in Europe it lays)
to a Catholic family, devout in praise.

Close to her mother, who taught her charity,
she fed those living in scarcity.

At eighteen, she answered her true calling:
joined a convent for a life of faith and belonging.

She moved to India to serve the poor,
and taught young girls that life offers more.

One day, she heard God—a call within a call!—
care for the most needy in Calcutta's walls.

Dressed in her white-blue sari for a lifetime,
She aided the poor and sick as their numbers climbed.

Her calling turned into more concrete plans...
She opened a school and clinic, then began

a charity for those disabled and poor.
(Donations made it possible to help much more.)

Her concern and care were felt far and wide,
earning her the acclaimed Nobel Peace Prize.

When in doubt, her empathy pushed her through,
using her skills to fuel feelings—can-do!

She's a true symbol of love, compassion, and grace.
With *pyaar*, you too can help the problems we face.

DO YOU KNOW THESE WORDS?
Devout: Having deep religious feelings
Scarcity: A shortage
Acclaimed: Praised enthusiastically
Pyaar: Love in Hindi

CAN YOU FIND THESE OBJECTS?
Holy cross - 2
Schoolhouse
Heart

SANIA MIRZA
Smashing Tennis Champion
Born November 15, 1986
Telangana, India

Forehand, backhand, ace, doubles, match point—
Sania's fierce tennis skills don't disappoint.

Hyderabad is her home from childhood days.
Raised Muslim, she loves tennis in all ways.

School is where she felt the freest of free!
(A girls' school is where she pursued her dream.)

She started tennis at the sweet age of six,
with her dad by her side and coaching her tricks.

Dedicated to tennis naturally,
she learned from her losses enjoyably.

She started in singles—a top 100 player—
but injury led her to be a doubles slayer.

When challenged by career, she stayed strong,
voicing her dress and success are not wrong.

Awarded with medals: bronze, silver, and gold,
six Grand Slams, Asian Games—there's more to be told!

She plays with grit and a *majabhoot* groundstroke,
swift velocity, and angles that smoke.

A positive influence when off the court,
she's a UN Ambassador for women's support.

She's a voice for challenging the status quo,
a voice for all girls: show the world what you know!

DO YOU KNOW THESE WORDS?
Majabhoot: Strong, powerful in Hindi
Swift: Happening quickly

CAN YOU FIND THESE OBJECTS?
Tennis racquet - 2
Tennis ball
Gold medal

SHAKUNTALA DEVI
Mathematical Mastermind
Born November 4, 1929 | Died April 21, 2013
Karnataka, India

Equations, cubes, roots, and puzzles—oh my!
Shakuntala's a genius, a one-of-a-kind.

Karnataka is where she was born and raised.
Poverty meant her schooling was constrained.

She traveled with her father, a circus trainer,
learned math skills as a card trick entertainer.

Her father knew a math whiz was here!
She had *kaushal* to compute with no fear.

He took her on road shows to reveal her gift,
showed how women and math are perfectly fit.

She attained worldly fame by reaching for the sky,
multiplied long numbers in the blink of an eye.

When questioned, she trusted her math ability.
Computers could not beat her capability.

The "Human Computer" was her new title . . .
She refused it—the mind is vast and vital.

In the Guinness Book of World Records she is named:
the fastest math calculation she has claimed.

A role model to girls in a STEM path,
she proves women, too, are gifted in math.

So dream of experiments and formulas, too.
With math, there is nothing you cannot do.

DO YOU KNOW THESE WORDS
Constrained: Overly controlled
Kaushal: Skill in Hindi
Attained: Reached, achieved successfully

CAN YOU FIND THESE OBJECTS?
Playing cards - 4
Computer
Brain

THE SHAKTI WITHIN YOU

Your shakti is the strength, energy, and power that lives inside you. It can appear as one or more qualities, interests, or abilities.
Think about your powerful qualities, interests, or abilities. What are they? Draw objects and symbols that represent them in the heart below.

WORDS TO LIVE BY

Find the empowering hindi words listed below and then complete the affirmation sentences to discover how you already live by these words. You can find the definition of each word in the poems in this book.

```
Y S M E N B Z Y H A T H E E V
Z A A V A I D L V D J N N S I
Z P C V P X D L H G Q K C A S
G A S B B P G A B W F O R I H
M N S A Y Y I H R H B U G M V
T E X A T R F S K A T H O R A
K O A B Y Y X O K A U J Y D A
Q R O A P A A J H V C E N R S
A C C H C T F C T F M P N G X
W E Y C B V X L C M N I E L P
W K R Q G A G W P Y O Z M L F
L C X E W G J A P J W C X T H
K D Q R G I B A U W U Y L S I
S X Q M D J C D M R C U L H X
I N N B O L U U I X O G E V H
```

Avaaz	Chaturai	Dhairya
Hathee	Josh	Kathor
Majabhoot	Nidar	Pyaar
Sapane	Satya	Vishvaas

✳ I won't give up. I am hathee to _____.

✳ Fear can't stop me. I am nidar when I _____.

✳ I will reach my goals. I have a sapane that I will one day _____.

✳ What I say matters. My avaaz is _____.

✳ I am resilient. When I _____, I remain kathor.

✳ I have pyaar for all of me, especially _____.

About the Author

Shetal Shah grew up to the sounds of Bollywood and the delicious smells of her mother's Indian cooking in the suburbs of New York City. As a second-generation Indian-American, Shetal hoped to one day see more stories of girls like her fill the shelves of local bookstores. A former educator, Shetal taught world history in both public and private all-girls schools, where she witnessed how curriculum and literature inclusive of women from diverse backgrounds can have a positive impact on girls' self-esteem, identity development, and belonging. Shetal also developed and led numerous educator workshops, presenting at national conferences covering topics on pedagogy and diversity and inclusion. She lives in Atlanta, Georgia, with her husband and her two young boys. *Shakti Girls* is her first book. You can follow her at shetal-shah.com and on Instagram @shetal.shah.writes.

About the Illustrator

Kavita Rajput is an illustrator and surface designer based in New York City, USA. Growing up in Mumbai, India, Kavita was constantly surrounded by Indian art, be it in the form of rangoli, henna, colorful fabrics or the vibrant sets of Bollywood movies. An only child, she often took to sketching and painting during her free time. A graduate of the London Business School, she worked in finance for almost a decade till an after-work watercolor class at the New York Academy of Art took her back to her childhood passion. Shakti Girls is Kavita's third book. You can follow her on Instagram: @kavita_rajput and on her website: www.kavitarajput.com.

Made in the USA
Middletown, DE
13 October 2023

40737002R00020